Caring Koala Teaches Self-Care

by William Anthony

Minneapolis, Minnesota

Credits

All images are courtesy of Shutterstock.com, unless otherwise specified. With thanks to Getty Images, Thinkstock Photo, and iStockphoto. Cover – InstaMovie. 4–5 – wowomnom. 6–7 – alinabuphoto, Riccardo Mayera. 8–9 – MaLija. 10–11 – Black-Photogaphy, ifong. 12–13 – Littlekidmoment. 14–15 – PR Image Factory. 18–19 – Monkey Business Images, Daisy Daisy. 20–21 – Jihan Nafiaa Zahri, Rawpixel.com. 22–23 – David Tadevosian.

Library of Congress Cataloging-in-Publication Data is available at www.loc.gov or upon request from the publisher.

ISBN: 978-1-63691-849-5 (hardcover)
ISBN: 978-1-63691-854-9 (paperback)
ISBN: 978-1-63691-859-4 (ebook)

© 2023 Booklife Publishing
This edition is published by arrangement with Booklife Publishing.

North American adaptations © 2023 Bearport Publishing Company. All rights reserved. No part of this publication may be reproduced in whole or in part, stored in any retrieval system, or transmitted in any form or by any means, electronic, mechanical, photocopying, recording, or otherwise, without written permission from the publisher.

For more information, write to Bearport Publishing, 5357 Penn Avenue South, Minneapolis, MN 55419. Printed in the United States of America.

Contents

Today's Class 4
Introducing Self-Care 6
Looking After You 8
Let's Eat! 10
Be Mindful 12
Yoga 14
Time to Meditate 16
Get Active 18
Help Me, Help You 20
You Did It! 22
Glossary 24
Index 24

Introducing Self-Care

Today's calm class is all about self-care.

Have you ever heard of self-care?

Looking After You

It is very important to keep your body healthy. Did you know that your body's health can **affect** how you think and feel?

Here's a list of things you can do to care for your body.

Exercise

Eat healthy food

Get the right amount of sleep

These things will help your mind stay healthy, too!

Let's Eat!

Eating healthy foods will give your body the right kind of **energy**. And your brain needs good food just as much as your body does.

Be Mindful

Mindfulness is another important part of self-care. It is about **focusing** only on what you are doing right now. This can help you feel calm and less worried.

Here are some steps for practicing mindfulness.

1. Grab something to drink.

2. Focus on your drink.

3. Is it hot or cold?

4. What flavor is it?

5. Does it taste good?

Yoga

Yoga is an exercise for your body and mind together. It's perfect for self-care!

During yoga, you make shapes with your body called poses. You also focus on your breathing.

1 Stand up straight.

2 Stand on one foot.

3 Place your other foot above or below your knee.

4 Bring your hands together above your head.

5 Breathe slowly. Focus on each breath.

Here are some steps for a yoga pose.

Time to Meditate

Self-care also helps people deal with **stress**. Meditation is one way to do this. It can help you relax. Let's try it!

1. Close your eyes.
2. Imagine an object.
3. Focus on its shape and colors.
4. Think about nothing else.
5. When you feel relaxed, open your eyes.

Get Active

Exercise is very important for keeping your body healthy.

But did you know that exercise keeps your mind healthy, too?

Help Me, Help You

Helping others can make you feel good, too! However, it can be hard to make other people feel better when you don't feel happy yourself.

Self-care is a good way to help yourself feel positive. When you feel good, it is easier for you to help someone else.

21

You Did It!

Good job! Caring for yourself is important!

I ♥ Self-Care

You may have to try different forms of self-care to find what feels best for you.

Thank you for coming to my calm class. Remember, you can always come back if you need a reminder lesson!

Glossary

affect to cause something to change

energy the power to be active and do things

focusing giving your full attention to something

healthy when the body and mind are working at their best

mental health how well we feel in our minds

mind the part of a person that thinks, feels, and remembers

stress something that causes strong feelings of worry

Index

body 7–10, 14, 18–19
brain 10–11
breathing 14–15
endorphins 19
food 9–11
health 5, 7–11, 18–19
mind 5, 9, 14, 18
sleep 9
stress 16